Oval Cutters adjust from 3/4" to 6 1/2" and have replaceable blades. Use with a self-healing mat. Ovals may be used to make all kinds of animals and characters.

Craft Knife & Mat. Use a craft knife and a self-healing mat to make neat rounded shapes and interior cuts. Use with care, the blade is extremely sharp.

Personal Handle Cutter is used to make straight cuts. The mini size makes it perfect for trimming photos and small pieces of paper.

Personal Slide Cutter is used to make straight cuts in photos, paper and cardstock up to 12" wide with a safe replaceable blade. The base is ruled for accuracy.

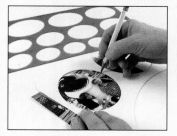

Template & Stencil. Trace template or stencil on front of photo and cut inside line or trace on wrong side of photo using a light box or holding photo on a window.

Scissors. Use scissors to cut straight lines and simple shapes. Lubricate by cutting through waxed paper and sharpen by cutting through extra-fine sandpaper.

Wavy Edge Scissors. By turning scissors over, most will cut more than one design. Do not cut to the very end of blades. Use wavy edge scissors to cut shapes, frames, corners and borders.

Table of Contents

Red–Eye Remover – Dot red eyes with remover pen.

Before   After

Pet–Eye Remover – Dot pet eyes with remover pen.

Before   After

SUPPLIER
Red-Eye & Pet-Eye Removers   **Flashpoint**, P.O. Box 2682, Fair-Lawn, NJ 07410

Dog House – 1 1/2" circle photo cut with Zig Zag scissors, Silhouette dog photo, 4" die cut doghouse, 3" die cut dog, 3 1/2" die cut bone, 3" die cut sun, Grass cut with scallop scissors

Practice with Your Camera

2 Feet

4 Feet

8 Feet

Practice makes perfect. Experiment with photos taken at different distances from the subject. You'll develop a feel for taking a photo that showcases the subject to the best advantage.

Have Fun with Your Photos

Make photos fun. Use alphabet templates to cut letter shapes that highlight the subject and help tell the photo story.

Better Photos...

Close–Up to Capture the Subject
Fill the Frame

Get as close as possible to capture the subject without losing the background setting.

Impromptu Photos Capture Mood & Emotion

Action Shots – Always have a camera ready to take candid photos that record rare moments.

Eye Level is Best –

For the best portraits of people and pets, take the photo at eye level.

Underwater Cameras –

Try using a disposable for unique action shots.

Hints, Tips and Tricks

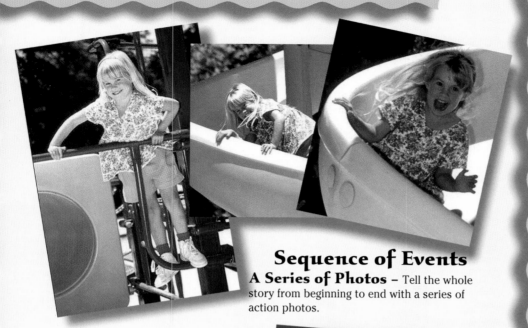

Part of image cut off

Image centered in frame

Sequence of Events

A Series of Photos – Tell the whole story from beginning to end with a series of action photos.

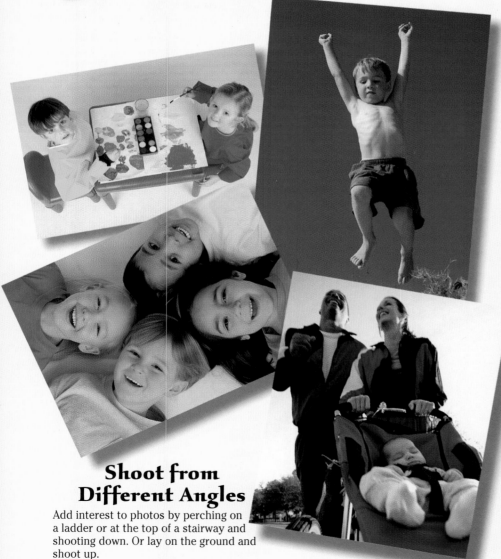

Use Correct Speed Film

1000 for Night

400 for Action

100 for Daylight

Shoot from Different Angles

Add interest to photos by perching on a ladder or at the top of a stairway and shooting down. Or lay on the ground and shoot up.

Perfect Cropping Every Time

Too Much Background –
The subject is lost in a sea of background.

Too Close –
The subject appears to be trapped in a tiny box.

Just Right –
The perfect balance of subject and background makes the photo perfect.

Bump Out - Bump out and accent the photo subject by cutting away or silhouetting part of the photo and leaving part of the background.

Silhouette - Cut around photo subject removing all uninteresting or distracting background.

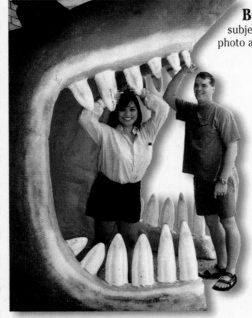

2 into 1 - To add interest to a landscape or scenery photo, cut and glue a silhouette to the foreground.

Cropping

Formal Portrait - Multiple rectangle or oval mats complement formal portraits. The wedding photo was cut into an oval and placed on an oval Magenta mat. Cut a White mat with scallop wavy edge scissors. Add White mat and a plain Teal mat to complete a formal portrait.

Group Photos - Because there is so much going on in group photos, cutting away uninteresting background can cut down on clutter.

Original Photo

Cropped Photo - Crop and round corners to soften.

Silhouette Photo

Vary the Shape... Change the Effect

Choose a Shape that works well with the photo and complements theme of the album page.

To Crop or Not to Crop

Not all photos are picture perfect. Many photos can be improved by cropping or cutting photos to remove distracting details or uninteresting background and direct the viewer's eye to the subject. Cropping adds interest and makes room on album pages for more photos. Think twice before cropping old photos. Historical items such as cars, buildings, houses or clothing styles tell a story and places photo subject in a certain time or place. If you are reluctant to crop Black and White historical photos or one-of-a-kind color photos, copy both on a color copier and crop the copies. Before you begin cropping, be sure you have back up copies or negatives of photos stored in a safe place.

Photo Tricks

A Prize Catch

Combine 2 Photos into 1 – Cut a silhouette of an enlargement of the same photo and glue over matching portion of matted photo.

Postage Stamp Frames – Put a unique stamp on your favorite photo. Glue a frame of colorful cancelled postage stamps to the mat.

Happy Faces – Create a circle of love. Cut a circle close around photo subject. To make rick-rack design, turn jumbo scallop wavy edge scissors upside-down and cut Light Green mat. Turn scissors right side up and cut Dark Green mat.

Punch a Bunch – Make your favorite guy a star. 3" square photo, 3¼" square mat, 4¾" Red mat with ½" star punches, 5" Blue mat

Corner Decor – Hearts corner the love. 3⅛" x 3¾" photo, 3½" x 4" Gold mat, 4⅛" x 4¾" White mat cut with Jumbo scallop scissors, 4⅞" x 5½" Blue, ¾" heart punch corners

Lacy Frame. A lacy frame lets the love shine through. 2" x 2¾" photo, 3" x 3¾" colored mat and 2¾" x 3½" White mat cut with Traditional scissors, ¼" heart punch

Frames

Waves - Capture the fun of a day at the beach. 4" x 5" photo, 4½" x 5½" mat, Two waves cut with Jumbo Scallop scissors

PAGE IDEA !

Bugs and Butterflies

Bugs & Butterflies Page - Outdoor fun with dad. 2 photos, Background paper, Butterfly and flower die cuts, Butterfly sticker, Permanent pens, Deckle edge scissors

House - Fill a house with love. 1¾" square photo, 2½" square for house, ½" x 1¼" rectangle for chimney, 1½" x 3" triangle cut with Dragonback scissors, 7⁄16" heart punch

Sticker Stuff - A young beauty, fresh and new as spring. 3¾" x 5⅝" photo, 4" x 5⅞" Green mat, 4½" x 6⅜" Light Green mat cut with Scallop scissors,1½" rabbit, ⅝" eggs, 1" daffodil and ½" grass stickers

Add a Little… Add a Lot

Plain - 3" square photo, 3⅝" square Yellow mat

Wavy Frame - 3" square photo, 3⅝" square Yellow mat, 4⅛" square Green mat cut with Provincial scissors

Add Corners, Too - Bloom where you are planted. 3" square photo, 3⅝" square Yellow mat, 4⅛" square Green mat, 4⅝" square Brown mat cut with Provincial scissors, 5⅛" square Tan mat, Sunflowers cut with 1" star and ⅝" circle punches

Improve Your Photos

Silhouette Part of Your Photo

Remove cluttered background

Highlight the subject

Show off details

Silhouette

BOO! Baby – Peter pumpkin eater is filled with Halloween fun. Silhouette photo, Three 2½" Orange circles for pumpkin, Face cut from 1¼" Black circle, Green leaves cut with Alps canyon cutters, 2⅛" x 1⅛" Orange rectangle for sign, 'BOO!' sticker, Black marker

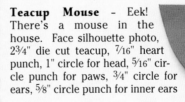

Teacup Mouse – Eek! There's a mouse in the house. Face silhouette photo, 2¾" die cut teacup, ⁷⁄₁₆" heart punch, 1" circle for head, ⁵⁄₁₆" circle punch for paws, ¾" circle for ears, ⁵⁄₈" circle punch for inner ears

Watermelon – Just one more bite! Silhouette photo, 4" Green, White and Red circles for watermelon, ⁷⁄₁₆" heart punch for seeds

Photos

Silhouettes Improve Your Photos

Just Swinging – Nothing's as free as swinging from a tree! Silhouette photo, Brown tree trunk cut with Deckle scissors, 9 Green circles for leaves, Rope cut with Mini Scallop scissors, grass cut with Jumbo Scallop scissors, $7/16$" heart punch and $1/4$" star punch for flowers

Reindeer – He's a 'deer' boy! Face silhouette photo, 3" die cut wreath backed with Red paper, $4\frac{1}{2}$" die cut reindeer, $3/4$" heart punch for inner ears

Rabbit in a Hat – No magic, just a sweet bunny. Face silhouette photo, $2\frac{1}{4}$" die cut top hat, 1" circle for head, $5/16$" circle punch for paws, $1\frac{1}{4}$" and $3/4$" heart punches for ears, $1/2$" bow punch

Learning to Walk Page – Brother lends a helping hand. Silhouette cut photo, Photo, Design Originals Cloud background paper, Red die cut wagon, Red borders cut with Deckle edge scissors, Permanent marker

My First Big Wheel Page – Every boy loves wheels! Silhouette cut photos, Photos, Design Originals House and Tree background paper, Farm animal stickers, Green mats cut with deckle edge scissors, Permanent marker

All Star Player Page – Ready for the big game. Silhouette cut photo, Photo, White background paper, $1/2$" star punch, Blue and Grey mats cut with Deckle edge scissors, Red, Black and Blue permanent markers

Circle Cutter...

Ball Pit Page – Never lose your sense of childhood wonder! 6" circle photo, 6½" circle mat, ⅜" strips cut with Stamps scissors for border, 1¼" circles for balls, ⅝" sticker letters

PAGE IDEA !

Circle Cutters are available in different styles and sizes. Some cut only one size while others are adjustable. Try them out and choose the one that most often suits your circle cutting needs.

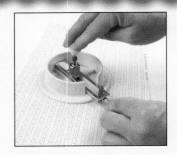

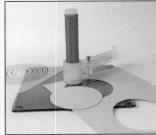

Hot Air Balloon – Up and away, the sky's the limit. Silhouette photo, 1½" square cut with Mini Scallop scissors for basket, Two 2¾" circles one cut with Cloud scissor for balloon, ⁷/₁₆" heart punch, ¹/₁₆" x 3" strips for rope

Sun – She's my sunshine, my only sunshine. 2½" circle photo, 4" circle cut with Zig Zag scissors, 4" circle with notches for rays, Black marker

Use the Whole Circle

Rattle – Babies are love. 1¼" circle photo, 1⅜" circle mat, 1¾" circle for rattle top, ⅝" and 1¼" circles for rattle bottom, bow sticker

Blue Ribbon – Mom's a winner. 1½" circle photo, 1⅝" circle mat, 2" Blue circle, ¾" x 3" strips for ribbons

Sunflower – Daddy's little flower. 1¾" circle photo, 2" circle mat, ¾" heart punch, 2" circle for leaves and stem

TIP

Use a circle cutter or template to cut out the important part of your photo. Then highlight the special image with a uniquely shaped mat.

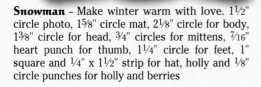

Snowman – Make winter warm with love. 1½" circle photo, 1⅝" circle mat, 2⅛" circle for body, 1⅜" circle for head, ¾" circles for mittens, ⁷/₁₆" heart punch for thumb, 1¼" circle for feet, 1" square and ¼" x 1½" strip for hat, holly and ⅛" circle punches for holly and berries

Chick – Remember a fun day at the farm. 1¾" circle photo, 2¼" circle for body, 1¼" circle for head, ⅛" circle punch for eye, 1¼" circle for tail, ⅛" x 1" strips for legs, ⅝" circle punch cut with notches for feet

Apple – He's the apple of Grandma's eye. 2⅛" circle photo, 1⅝" mat, 2⅛" circle for apple, 1" circle for leaf

Circle Cutter...

Sunshine Page - Fill a page with the warmth of the sun. Silhouette photo, Photos cut to fit a 4¼" circle, 1¼" flower and ⅝" circle punches for flowers, 3" Orange and Yellow circles for sun, ¾" letter stickers

You Are My Sunshine

Each Spring Our Family Goes on a Special Nature Retreat.

ROSE MARIE KILBER

PAGE IDEA !

Fish - Fishing for compliments. 1½" circle photo, 1⅝" circle mat, 2" circle body, 1½" circle for tail, 1½" circle for fins, ¼" circle punch for eye

Turtle - Hurray for the Turtle Team! 1½" circle photo, 1⅝" circle mat, 2" circle body, ¾" heart punch for head and feet

Balloon - Floating on a bubble of love. 1¼" circle photo, 1⅜" circle mat, 1⅞" circle for balloon, 1" circle for balloon neck, Wavy ruler

Tomato - Grandpa's newest farm hand. 1¾" circle photo, 2⅜" circle for tomato, 1¼" star punch, Paper for stem

Pumpkin - Posing pumpkin pals. 1½" circle photo, 1⅝" circle mat, Three 2" circles for pumpkin, 1" circle punch for leaves, paper for stem

Use the Whole Circle

TIP

Circle cutters make it fast and easy to trim and mat photos. Use the whole circle. Add embellishments with circles cut into halves or wedges.

Photo Birdhouse - He's my sweety bird. 2" circle photo, ¼" wide L for roof, ¼" x 2½" strip for pole, Two ¾" circles and ⁵/₁₆" circle punch for bird, Yellow marker

Photo Balloon - Love in flight. 2" circle photo, 1¼" circle photo, Black marker

Photo Rabbit - Easter fun for everyone. 2¾"circle photo, 1½" circle photo for head, 1½" circle photo for ears, ⁵/₈" circle punch for muzzle, ⅛" circle punch for eyes, ¾" circle photo for hands, 1½" circle photo for feet

Photo Fish - The prize catch. 2¼" circle photo for body, 2¼" circle photo for tail and lower fin, 2¼" circle photo for top fin, ⁵/₁₆" circle punch for lips, ¼" circle punch for eye

Photo Snowman - Bundle up for snowy fun. 2" circle photo for body, 1³/₈" circle photo for head, ⅛" circle punch for eyes and mouth, 1³/₈" circle and ¼" x 1½" strip with rounded ends for hat, ⁵/₁₆" circle punch for pompon, ¾" circle and ⁷/₁₆" heart punches for mittens, ¾" circles for feet, ¼" x 1⅓" strips and ⁵/₁₆" circle punch for scarf

Circles

Whole Circle

1/2 Circles

1/4 Circles

1/8 Circles

1/16 Circles

Stork Page - A special delivery. 2¾" x 4⅛" oval photo cut with Stamp scissors, 3" x 4½" oval for body, 1¼" circle for head, 1⅝" circle for beak, 1½" circle for tail, ⅛" x 4½" strip and ¾" star punch for legs and feet, Silhouette photo of baby, 3½" teardrop and ¾" heart punch for bag, 3½" heart cut with Stamp scissors, 4" Pink heart, ½" strips cut with Wavy scissors for borders, ⅝" sticker letters

PAGE IDEA !

OUR NEW ARRIVAL

Deborah Ann
7 Pounds 4 Ounces
March 17, 1998

Flower. A flower in the garden of love. 1⅛" circle photo, 1¼" and 1½" mats cut with Deckle scissors, Leaves cut with Jumbo Scallop scissors

Christmas Ornament - Holiday happiness. 1⅝" circle photo, 1¾" circle mat, 2⅜" circle for ornament, ½" square cut with Mini Scallop scissors for ornament top, ¼" and ⁵⁄₁₆" punches for hanger

Use the Whole Circle

Spider - Creepy, crawly fun. 1⅛" circle photo, 2" circle for body, ⅞" circle for head, ⅛" circle punch for eyes, ⅛" wide L shapes for legs

Frog - Croakin' with happiness. 2⅜" circle photo, 2⅞" circle for body, 1½" circle for head, ⅝" and ¼" circle punch and ¾" Green circles for eyes, ⅛" circle punch for nose, 1½" circle for legs, ⅝" circle punch for feet

Sun - He's the light of my life. 1⅝" circle photo, 2⅝" circle for rays cut with V notches

Teapot - How about a tea party? 1⅝" circle photo, 2" circle for pot, ¾" White and 1⅛" Blue circles for handle, 2" circle for lid, ¼" circle punch for lid handle, 3⁄16" x 1¼" strip for base, 1⅜" circle for cup, 5⁄16" White and ⅝" Purple circles for cup handle, ⅛" x ¾" strip for cup base, 7⁄16" heart punch

Turkey - He's no turkey, he's my boy! 1⅝" circle photo, 2" circle for body, ⅞" circle for head, ⅛" x ⅝" strips for legs, ⅝" circle punch cut with notches for feet, ¼" triangle for beak, 7⁄16" heart punch for wattle, ¼" punch for nose, ⅛" circle punch for eyes, 1" circle for wings

Ladybug - Under the wings of love. 1½" circle photo, 1⅞" circle for body, 1⅞" circle for wings, ⅝" circle punch for head, ¼" circle punch for spots and antennae

Mouse - There's lots of fun in our house. $3\frac{1}{2}$" circle photo, 4" circle for body, $\frac{3}{4}$" and $1\frac{1}{4}$" circles for ears, $\frac{5}{16}$" circle punch for nose, $\frac{1}{4}$" circle punch for eye, $1\frac{1}{2}$" circle punch for tail

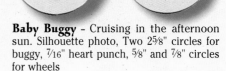

PAGE
IDEA
!

Baby Buggy - Cruising in the afternoon sun. Silhouette photo, Two $2\frac{5}{8}$" circles for buggy, $\frac{7}{16}$" heart punch, $\frac{5}{8}$" and $\frac{7}{8}$" circles for wheels

Home Run Page - Our baseball all star. Photos cut to fit a $6\frac{1}{2}$" circle, $3\frac{7}{8}$" x $5\frac{3}{8}$" rectangle photo, $4\frac{5}{8}$" x 6" mat cut with Seagull scissors, Wavy edge ruler, $\frac{3}{4}$" letter stickers, Red marker

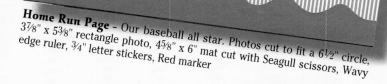

Ball Cap - Family fun at the baseball park. 3" circle photo, $3\frac{1}{2}$" circle for cap, $1\frac{3}{4}$" circle for bill, $\frac{5}{16}$" circle punch for button, $1\frac{1}{4}$" circle for ball, Red marker

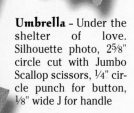

Umbrella - Under the shelter of love. Silhouette photo, $2\frac{5}{8}$" circle cut with Jumbo Scallop scissors, $\frac{1}{4}$" circle punch for button, $\frac{1}{8}$" wide J for handle

Use Parts of a Circle

Photo Sailboat - Watery fun in the summer sun. 4" circle photo for boat, 5" and 6" circle photos for sails, ¼" x 4" photo strip for mast, 1" circle photo for flag

Photo Flower - Shining bright in a garden of flowers 1½" circle photo, 1¾" Yellow circle, 2" circle photo for leaves and petals, ¼" x 2½" photo strip for stem

Photo Butterfly - On the wings of a warm summer day. Two 3" circle photos for wings, Body cut with Jumbo Scallop scissors, ¼" circle punch, Black marker

Photo Bird - She brings a song to my heart. 3" circle photo for body, 1¼" circle photo for head, ¼" circle punch for eye, 2½" circle photo for tail, ½" star punch for beak

Circle Cutter...

Welcome Spring

Caterpillar Page - The family welcomes spring. 1⅞" circle photos, 2¼" circles for caterpillar, 5/16" circle punch for antennae and feet, ¾" heart and ¼" circle punches for bow tie, 1¼" heart and ¼" circle punches for flowers, Wavy edge ruler for grass, ⅝" letter stickers

PAGE IDEA!

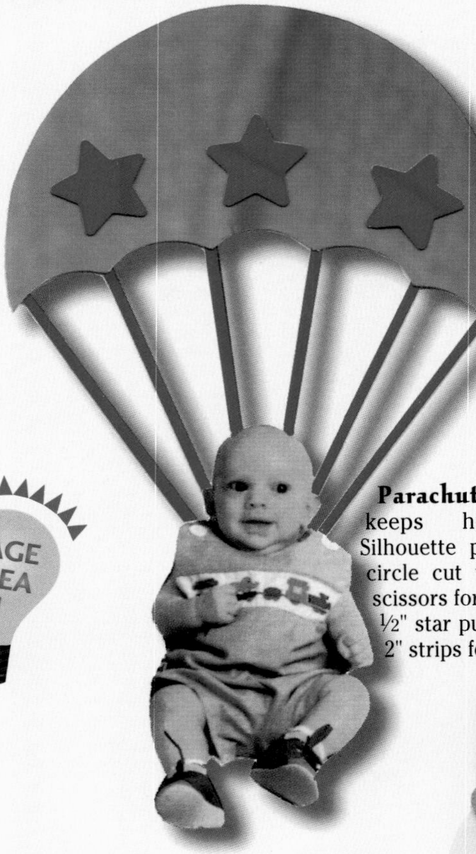

Parachute - Love keeps him safe. Silhouette photo, 2⅝" circle cut with Cloud scissors for parachute, ½" star punch, 1/16" x 2" strips for cords

Elephant - I love you thissss much! 1½" circle photo, 2¼" circle for body, 1½" circle for head, 1" and 1½" circles for ears, ¼" circle and ⅝" circle extended on one side to form a curved trunk, ⅝" x 1¼" rectangles for legs, ⅝" circle punch for feet, ⅝" x 1¼" rectangle of striped paper, ⅝" Blue square and ½" star punch for flag

Photo Star - My bright and shining star. 1⅛" circle photo, 1⅜" circle mat, 2" circle photo for rays

Toy Soldier - I surrender, you've captured my heart. 1⅞" oval photo, Two 2⅛" ovals for body and arms, ⅝" circle punch for hands and feet, 1⅛" circle for head, ⅜" x 1¼" strips for legs, ¾" x 1" rectangle for hat, ¾" circle for bill, ⅛" x ¾" strip for hat trim, ¼" circle punch for cheeks and buttons, ¾" heart punch for hat plume, ⅜" square cut with Stamp scissors for epaulets

Use Parts of a Circle

Circle Cutters come in many sizes. By using different sizes, you can use one photo to create several different effects and highlight different images.

Photo Tree - My favorite Christmas ornament. 2", 3" and 4" circle photos for tree, 2" circle photo for trunk, 7/16" star punch

Ball Player - Play ball! Face silhouette photo, 1¼" and ¾" circles and ⅛" circle punch for hat

Clown - My own little funny face. Face silhouette photo, 2¼" circle for hat, ¼" and 5/16" circle punches for pompons

Witch - She fills our lives with good spells. Face silhouette photo, Two 3" circles and ⅛" strip for hat

Santa - This hat's too tight! Face silhouette photo, 2¼" circle, ¼" x 1" strip and ¼" circle punch for hat

Three Peas in a Pod - The children fill our life with love. Silhouette photos, 5" circle for pod with slit, Small triangle for stem, 1½" circles for peas

Large Circle

Medium Circle

Small Circle

Original Photo

Perfect Ovals Every Time

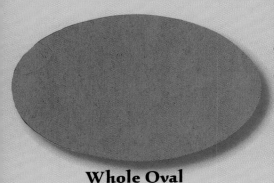

Whole Oval

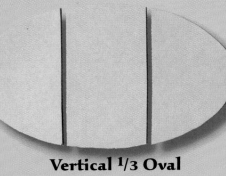

1/2 Oval

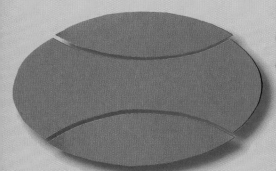

Vertical 1/3 Oval

Horizontal 1/3

Oval Cutters...

Oval Cutters adjust from ¾" to 6½" and have replaceable blades. Use with a self-healing mat. Ovals may be used to make all kinds of animals and characters.

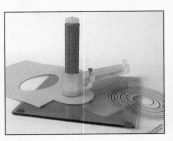

Rabbit Head – Hoppin' down the bunny trail. Silhouette photo, 2¼" x 3¾" oval for head, Heart sticker, Black marker, ¼" circle punch for eyes

Apple Core – An apple a day keeps baby at play. Silhouette photo, 2¼" x 3¾" Red and White ovals for apple, Scallop scissors, 7/16" heart punch for seeds, Trimmed ovals for leaf and stem

Mitten – Held in the warmth of love. Silhouette photo, 2¼" x 3¾" oval for mitten, 1½" heart for thumb, ¾" heart punch, ⅝" x 2½" strip with rounded ends for cuff

Baby in Flower – Nature's rarest bloom. Silhouette photo, 2¼" x 3¾" oval for flower, 2¼" x 3¾" oval for leaves

Fun with Bunnies, Flowers & Holidays

Hi-Hop Page – Easter brings spring fun. Photos, Design Originals Cloud background paper, Green paper, Easter stickers, Die cut eggs, Green mats cut with Deckle scissors, Permanent markers

Egg – She's our spring surprise. Silhouette photo, 3¾" x 4½" oval for egg, Victorian scissors, Baby stickers

Watermelon – I can't believe I ate the whole thing! Silhouette photo, 2¼" x 3¾" oval for melon, 2½" x 4" oval for rind, Black marker, Spoon sticker

Corn – He's helping with the harvest. Silhouette photo, 2¼" x 3¾" oval for corn, Two 2¼" x 3¾" ovals for shuck

Flower – My garden of flowers. 2¼" x 3¾" oval photos, 2¼" x 3¾" ovals for petals, ¼" strip for stem, 2¼" x 3¾" ovals for leaves.

TIP Oval cutters make it easy to create animals, critters and characters. Shape the body with ovals and add circles and strips to complete the design.

Penguin – 2¼" x 3¾" oval photo, 1½" circle for head, ¼" and ⁵⁄₁₆" circle punches for eyes, 2¼" x 3¾" oval for wings, 1" circle for feet

Bear – 2¼" x 3¾" oval photo, 1⅝" circle for head, ¾" circles for muzzles and ears, ⅝" circle punch for nose, ¼" and ⁵⁄₁₆" circle punches for eyes, 1" circles for paws, 1¼" circle for feet

Dog – 2¼" x 3¾" oval photo, 1⅜" circle for head, ⅝" circle punch for muzzle and nose, ⁵⁄₁₆" circle punch for tongue, ⅛" circle punch for eyes, 1½" circles for ears and feet, 1" circle for paws

Cat – 2¼" x 3¾" oval photo, 1⅜" circle for head, ⅝" circle punch for muzzle, ⁵⁄₁₆" circle punch for tongue and nose, ⅛" circle punch for eyes, 1¼" circles for ears and feet, 1" circle for paws

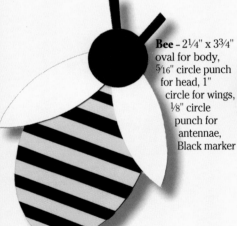

Bee – 2¼" x 3¾" oval for body, ⁵⁄₁₆" circle punch for head, 1" circle for wings, ⅛" circle punch for antennae, Black marker

Ant – 2¼" x 3¾" ovals for body, ⅛" strips for feet, ⅛" strips for antennae, Letter stickers

Lion – 2¼" x 3¾" oval photo, 2¼" x 4" oval for body, 1¼" circle for head, ⅝" circle punch for feet, muzzle, nose, mouth and mane, ⅛" circle punch for eyes, ⁵⁄₁₆" circle punch for ears

Pig – 2¼" x 3¾" oval photo, 2¼" x 4" oval for body, 1⅝" circle for head, ⅝" circle punch for snout, ⅛" circle punch for eyes and nose, ⅝" circle punch for ears and feet

Animals, Critters & Characters

Santa – 2¼" x 3¾" oval photo, 2½" x 4" oval for body, 1⅜" circle for head, 1⅝" circle for beard, ⅝" circle punch for moustache, 3¼" circle and ¼" x 1½" strip for hat, ⅝" circle punch for pompon, ⅛" circle punch for eyes, ⁵⁄₁₆" circle punch for nose and mouth, 1¼" circle for feet, ¾" circles and ⁷⁄₁₆" heart punch for mittens

Clown – 2¼" x 3¾" oval photo, 2¾" circle for head, 3¾" circle photo for sleeves, 3½" circle photo for hat, ⅝" circle punch for pompon, hands and hair, ⁵⁄₁₆" circle punch for nose, ⅛" circle punch for eyes, 1⅝" circle for feet

Photo Fish – 2¼" x 3¾" oval photo, ¾" heart punch for lips, Free form tail and fins

Fish – 2¼" x 3¾" ovals for body, fin and tail, ¾" heart punch for lips, Permanent marker

Ladybug – 2¼" x 3¾" oval for body and wings, ¾" heart punch for head, ⅛" circle punch for dots, ⅛" strips for antennae

Trick Photos

Original Photos – Make a trick photo by combining or merging several photos to create a more interesting composition.

Combined Photos - A walrus hug!

Original Photos

Combined Photos – A fairy princess on a zebra!

Caterpillar – Peaks scissors, $5/8$" circle punch for photos and body sections, $3/4$" circles for heads, $1/4$" circle punch for legs, Black marker

Stick People – Jumbo Wave and Bow Tie scissors, $7/16$" heart punch, $5/8$" circle punch for photos, 2" circles for dresses, $3/8$" squares for shirts, $3/8$" x $1/2$" rectangles for overalls, Black marker

Flowers – $3/4$" circle photos, $7/8$" circles for mats, $1\,1/4$" circles cut with notches for petals, $1/8$" x 1" strips for stems, $5/8$" circle punch for leaves, Scallop scissors for grass

Train – $3/4$" circle photos, Silhouette photo, Dragonback scissors for track, $1\,1/4$" x $2\,1/2$" rectangle for engine, $1\,1/4$" square and 1" photo for cab, $1\,5/8$" circle for roof, $5/16$" circle punch for light, $1\,1/4$" x 2" rectangles and $3/4$" heart punch for cars, $1\,1/4$" and $7/8$" circles for wheels, $3/4$" x 1" rectangle and $1/2$" star punch for flag, $7/8$" cloud punch for smoke,

Borders

Balloons – ⅝" circle punch for photos, 1" and ¾" circles for balloons, Jumbo Scallop scissors, Black marker

Hearts – ¾" heart punch for photos, 1¼" and ⁷⁄₁₆" heart punches, Victorian scissors

Turtle – ⅞" circle photos, 1⅛" circles for shells, ¾" heart punch for head, ⁷⁄₁₆" heart punch for tail, ⁵⁄₁₆" circle punch for feet, Black marker

Ornaments – 1" circle photos, ½" strip of striped paper, ⅜" square trimmed with Mini Scallop scissors for ornament tops, ¼" and ⁵⁄₁₆" circle punches for hangers, Holly punch, ¼" circle punch

Borders... A Great Way To Use Scraps

Punch mats from colored paper.

Photos. Punch faces from photos.

Glue faces to mats and assemble borders. Embellish with punches. stickers and markers.

PAGE IDEA!

3 Little Flowers Page – 4¾" x 6¾" photo, 1¼" circle photos with notches for flowers, ⅝" circle punch for flower centers and leaves, ⅛" x 1½" photo strips for stems, Green photo scraps cut with Jumbo Scallop scissors for grass, 5¼" x 7¼" White mat cut with Victorian scissors, 5½" x 7½" Blue mat, 6" x 8" Yellow mat, ½" letter stickers

Panorama Pop-Up Pages...

Photo. Plan pop-up page. Cut out silhouette photo.

Arch. Cut arch using pattern, fold. Glue arch and silhouette photo on page making sure photo is inside page when closed.

Pop-Up Halloween Page - Oh, what a spooky bunch! Photos, Silhouette photo, Design Originals Pumpkin and Candy paper, White cardstock, Black and Orange markers
Make 2 long panorama base strips from cardstock. Cut pumpkins, candy and borders from Pumpkin and Candy paper. Glue photos and pop-up in place. Journal and make stitches with marker.

Finish. Glue mats and photos in place. Add journaling, stickers, die cuts and other embellishments.

Pop-Up Card

Christmas Card - Popping up to wish you a Merry Christmas! Group silhouette photo, 7" x 11" piece of White cardstock, 5" x 6½" piece of Red paper, 4½" x 6" piece of Red/White stripe paper cut with Jumbo Scallop scissors, 4½" die cut tree, ½" star punch, 5/16" circle punch, Narrow strip cut with Jumbo Scallop scissors for tree trim, 1¼" holly punch, ¼" circle punch, 5/8" sticker letters
Follow diagram to cut pop-up tabs for tree and photo. Glue the long side of the tab to pop-up and short sides to card.

— FOLD —

FLAP

Large

Medium

Small

Extra Small

Strip Base Patterns

FOLD

FOLD

FLAP

Large Arch Base

Medium Arch Base

Small Arch Base

FOLD

FLAP

FOLD

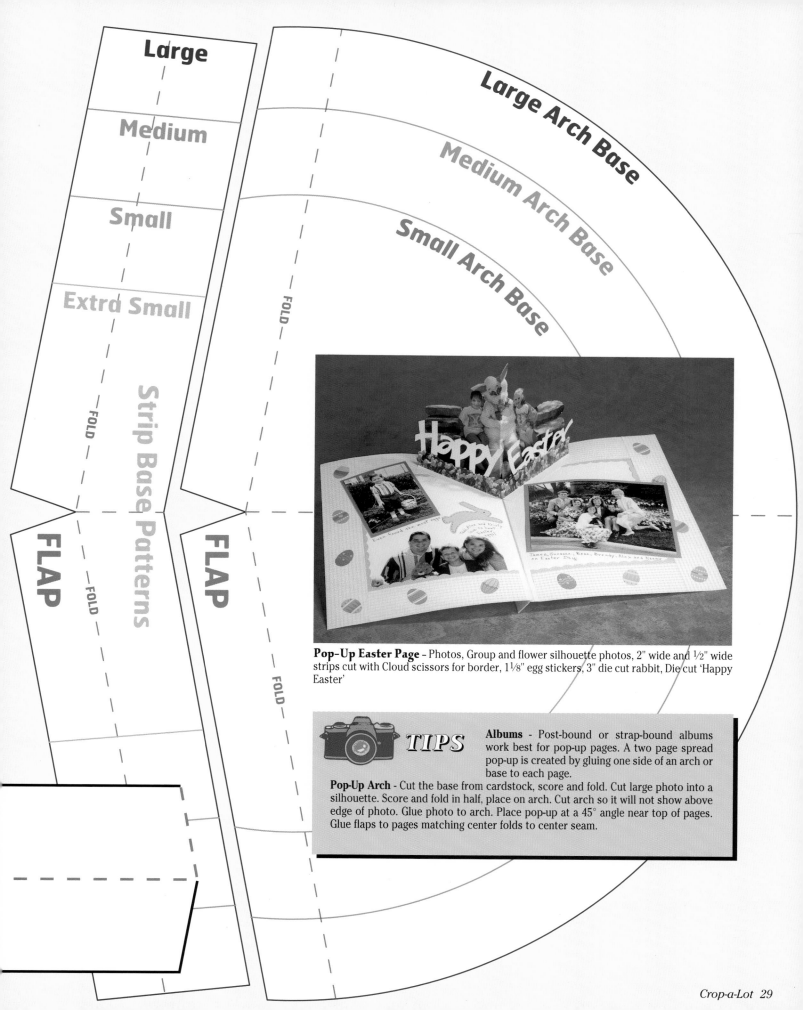

Pop–Up Easter Page – Photos, Group and flower silhouette photos, 2" wide and ½" wide strips cut with Cloud scissors for border, 1⅛" egg stickers, 3" die cut rabbit, Die cut 'Happy Easter'

TIPS

Albums - Post-bound or strap-bound albums work best for pop-up pages. A two page spread pop-up is created by gluing one side of an arch or base to each page.

Pop-Up Arch - Cut the base from cardstock, score and fold. Cut large photo into a silhouette. Score and fold in half, place on arch. Cut arch so it will not show above edge of photo. Glue photo to arch. Place pop-up at a 45° angle near top of pages. Glue flaps to pages matching center folds to center seam.

How to Make a Photo Puzzle

Photos. Gather several photos with the same theme.

Cut photo shapes to fit on background.

Finish. Write journaling on colored paper, cut with decorative scissors and glue in place.

Stained Glass

Trace a symmetrical pattern on back of photo. Cut out.

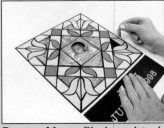

Reassemble on Black cardstock leaving ⅛" gap between pieces. Complete with colored paper.

PAGE IDEA!

Farm Page – Grandpa's farm is fun! 4⅝" heart photo, 5" heart mat, 3" x 5" rectangle cut with Jumbo Scallop scissors, ⅝" letter stickers
Place photos and arrange until pleased. Crop photos until page is completely covered.

Mountain High Page – I love a Rocky Mountain high. 3⅝" x 5⅝" photo, 5⅝" x 7⅛" Green mat cut with Zipper scissors, 3⅞" x 5⅞" Yellow mat, ⅛" wide Yellow strips, ⅝" sticker letters
Place photos and arrange until pleased. Crop photos with straight diagonal cuts and cover seams with Yellow strips.

JASON
JULY 7, 1998

Stained Glass Page – Make an extra special page for an extra special child. 4⅛" square photo, 9¼" square of Black cardstock, Colored paper

PAGE IDEA!

Layered Photos

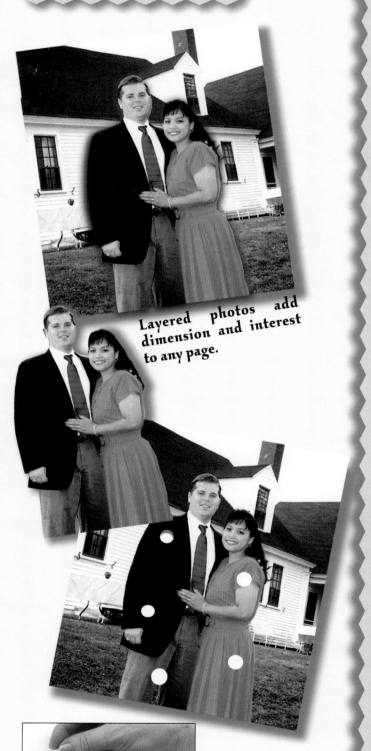

Layered photos add dimension and interest to any page.

Pop-Up Subject - Mat one photo, cut a silhouette from a second photo and apply with foam dots.

PAGE IDEA !

Photo Scraps

Our Family Page - Our house is filled with love. Face silhouette photos, 4¾" x 9¼" Green rectangle cut with Jumbo Scallop scissors, 8" x 9¼" Blue rectangle, 5¾" Brown square, 1¼" heart punch and 1" x 2" Brown rectangle for house, Blue L shape cut with Jumbo Scallop scissors for roof, 1¼" x 2½" Red rectangle for door, 1¼" White and 1½" Red squares for window, 1¾" circle for sun, 1½" circle for rays, ¾" and 1" circle and ⁵⁄₁₆" circle punch for bird, 1¼" x 2⅜" Blue and 1¼" x 1½" Red rectangles for Dad, 6½" circle ¾" heart punch for Mom, ⅞" x 1¼" Blue and ⅞" x ¾" striped rectangles for Baby, 5" circle and ⁷⁄₁₆" heart punch for Girl, 1 x 1½" Blue and ¾" x 1" striped rectangles for Boy, ½" and 1" letter stickers

New Home Page - A new home is filled with wonderful possibilities. 4⅛" square photo, 4¾" square Black mat cut with Victorian scissors, 5⅜" square striped mat, 6" square Black mat, 1½" leaf punch, Photo scraps for large letters, ¾" letter stickers Use soft pencil to draw large letters on thin paper. Turn paper over and trace letters. Glue small photo scraps to cover letters completely, cut out following pencil lines.

PAGE IDEA !

Photo Quilts

PAGE IDEA!

Baby Girl Quilt Page - Make a patchwork of love. 2½" square photos, Blue check paper to cover album page, 2½" squares of Pink check paper, 1¼" heart punch, ½" letter stickers

PAGE IDEA!

Quilt Page - Family members are patches in the quilt of life. Photos cut in quilt pattern, Background paper, Button and needle die cuts, Letter stickers

Photo Puzzles

PAGE IDEA!

Horse Page - Just horsing' around. Photos cropped in puzzle piece shapes, 6" square mat, 3" die cut boot, 8½" x 11" piece and ⅝" circle of Brown paper and ¼" circle punch for rope, Brown marker, ¾" letter stickers For each loop in rope, punch ¼" circle near edge of paper. Draw loops around circles with curving rope between loops. Draw slash marks with marker. Cut out rope. Glue ⅝" circle for knot and small Brown triangles for ends of rope.

PAGE IDEA!

Texas Page - Outstanding in their field. Photos cut to fit star and Texas shapes, Bluebonnet die cuts, Letter stickers, Permanent marker

And More...

Tree Page -
Favorite people fill the tree of life. Silhouette photos, Leaf shape photos, Silhouette flower photos for ground, 6½" die cut tree

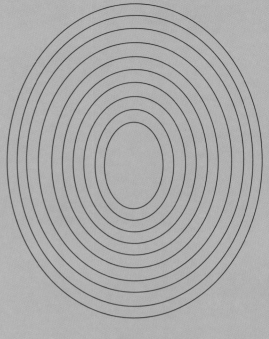

PAGE IDEA !

Puzzle-Up Flowers Page -
Special friends make my life bloom. Green photo scraps cut with Jumbo Scallop scissors for grass, 2¼" and 2½" circle photos for leaves, 1¼" heart photos, 3" circle of pieced photos for flower center, 2½" circle photo for bird, ⅜" x 4" and ⅜" x 6" Green strips for stems, 1½" Red hearts for petals, 2" Yellow circle, 1¼" Blue hearts for petals, 2¾" circle for bird body, 1¼" circle for bird head, 2½" circle for tail, ¼" x 8" strips for legs, ½" star punch for feet, ⅝" letter stickers

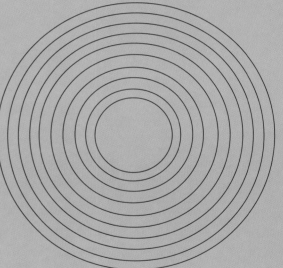

PAGE IDEA !

Templates. If you don't have a circle or oval cutter, use the circle and oval patterns. Trace them on your photos or on colored paper for mats. Use the templates to make any of the circle or oval designs included in this book.

Never Throw Away Another

Tombstone - 2¼" x 3¾" oval for stone, ⅜" x 2⅝" strip for base, 1/16" and 5/16" circle punches, ⅝" circle and 1¼" circle cut with Jumbo Scallop scissor for bat, Letter stickers

Angel - Face silhouette photo, 6" x 3" circles for dress and sleeves, 5/16" circle punch for hands and feet, Curved strip of paper cut with Jumbo Scallop scissors for lace, ¾" circle for halo, ½" star punch, 2½" circle for wings

Buttons - 1¼" Blue circle, ⅛" circle punch, ¾" Red circle, 1/16" circle punch, ⅝" Green circle, Black marker

Watermelon Slice - 4" Green, 3½" White and 3¼" Rose circles, 7/16" heart punch for seeds

Tulip - Two 1⅞" circles for petals, Mini Scallop scissors and ¼" circle punch for stamen, 1¼" circle for leaves, 1¼" x 2" strip for stem

Patchwork Heart - 3⅜"Light Blue heart, 7/16" heart punch, Photo scraps to cover heart

Turtle - A cute little photo turtle accents a page. 3⅜" Brown circle, 3" Green circle, 1¼" heart punch for tail, feet and head

Grapes - Make a bunch of love. 1" circle photos, 1" circles for grapes, 1¼" circle for leaves, ¼" x 1¼" strip for stem